h

A division of Hodder Headline Limited

© Hodder Children's Books 2005
Published in Great Britain in 2005
by Hodder Children's Books
Text © Simon Whaley
Illustrations © Jennifer Graham
Design by Andrew Summers
Cover design: Hodder Children's Books

The right of Simon Whaley to be identified as the author of the
work has been asserted by him in accordance with the Copyright,
Designs and Patents Act 1988.

10 9 8 7 6 5 4 3 2

A catalogue record for this book is available from the British Library

ISBN: 0 340 90306 6

Printed by Bookmarque Ltd, Croydon, Surrey

The paper and board used in this paperback by Hodder Children's
Books are natural recyclable products made from wood grown in
sustainable forests. The manufacturing
processes conform to the environmental regulations of the country
of origin.

Hodder Children's Books
a division of Hodder Headline Limited
338 Euston Road
London NW1 3BH

Puppytalk

50 Ways To Make Friends With Your Puppy

Simon Whaley

h

A division of Hodder Headline Limited

When your puppy first comes to live with you she may feel worried about being in a strange place. When they're anxious, some puppies look for things to chew. Pretend to be a puppy and crawl around on your hands and knees, looking for things that your puppy might chew. When you find something, move it somewhere out of your puppy's reach.

Take four pairs of your dad's old socks and stuff three of the pairs, and one sock from the fourth pair into the sock you have left. Tie a knot in the top of this sock and hey presto! You've made a great toy to play 'fetch' or 'tug of war' with your puppy. Just make sure that you use OLD socks. Your dad won't be very happy if he has to walk around in bare feet!

Pretend you're at a dog show and make your very own jumps in the garden. Balance a spade or stick on two buckets to make a jump. Jump over, and from the other side of the jump call your puppy's name and say 'Over' to encourage him to do the same. Keep the top of the jump below the height of your puppy's shoulder. If your jump is too high your puppy could hurt himself. Make a rosette and award yourselves first prize.

Play hide and seek. Dogs are very good at finding people, and the police and mountain rescue teams use some breeds to help them track down people who are lost. See what your puppy can do by hiding somewhere in your bedroom or the living room. Keep calling your puppy's name until she finds you, and then give her a big hug when she does.

Some puppies are trained to help carry and fetch things for blind or deaf people. See if you can train your puppy to help you. At the end of the day, get your puppy to help you bring indoors any balls or other toys that you've been playing with. Tell your puppy to 'fetch' the balls and bring them to you, so you can put them in a box and take them inside.

Chocolate can give your puppy a tummy ache and make him very sick, so share your sweets with your friends instead. Only give your puppy special doggy chocolate that you can buy at pet shops.

When we talk to our puppies, they don't actually understand the words we say. Instead they listen for the sounds we use. So if you train your puppy to lie down when you say 'lay', he may get confused because it will sound similar to your command 'stay'. Make a list of all the commands that you might use when talking to your puppy to check that they all sound different.

Learn to whistle. Dogs have very good hearing, and they are much better than people at hearing high notes. Whistling uses these high notes and can be a good way to call your puppy to come to you. If you enjoy playing hide and seek, don't call your puppy's name - try whistling instead.

Whenever your puppy does something that you have asked him to do, always praise him. Give him a big stroke or a cuddle, and this will encourage him to do it again the next time you ask him. Don't train him to do anything naughty. If you do, it's you being naughty, not your puppy.

Puppies love investigating new things, and this includes the decorations hanging on your Christmas tree. Hang little bells on the lower branches so your puppy can nudge them with his nose and make them ring. Make sure glass baubles are out of his reach, and sweets should be hung high up so your puppy can't eat them before you do!

At first, your Mum and Dad may get a big cardboard box for your puppy to sleep in. They will fill it with newspaper and blankets to make it cosy. Examine the cardboard box closely and make sure there are no sharp staples that could hurt your puppy.

Make a puppy memory box. Puppies grow up very quickly and some are fully-grown when they are just a year old. Keep lots of things that will remind you of when your dog was a puppy, such as photographs, fur from his grooming brush and some of his baby teeth. Decorate a box with pictures of your puppy, write his name on it in big letters, and put all your puppy memories inside.

Is your puppy fast asleep? Like human babies, puppies need lots of sleep when they are little, so don't wake her up. She might be having a lovely dream about a game she was playing with you earlier. Let your puppy wake up when she's ready.

Dogs should be brushed once a week
to keep them looking nice and clean.
Be careful when brushing your puppy,
as she might not like it at first. Stroke
her with your hand along her back
first, and when she is used to this,
take a very soft brush and gently
stroke her with it. Always praise your
puppy and tell her how good she is
being as you brush her.

How do you know that your puppy is happy? Look at what she is doing. If she's wagging her tail, then she's happy. If she's wagging her tail and barking, then she's very happy!

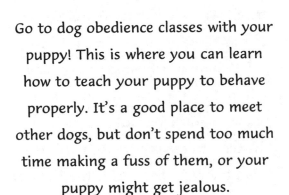

Go to dog obedience classes with your puppy! This is where you can learn how to teach your puppy to behave properly. It's a good place to meet other dogs, but don't spend too much time making a fuss of them, or your puppy might get jealous.

Carefully take a treat, hold it behind your back and hide it in one of your hands. Then hold both hands tightly out in front of you and your puppy, and ask him which hand you're hiding it in. Don't giggle when he starts tickling your hand with his tongue as he tries to eat the treat. When he's found the right hand, give the treat to your puppy, otherwise he might accidentally bite you in his excitement. Now go and wash your hands!

Your puppy's ancestors were wild dogs who caught their own prey and chewed the bones. This kept their teeth clean. You can ask for bones from your local butcher's shop - the best ones are called marrowbones. If you can't get a bone, you may have to buy a special toothbrush and toothpaste. Let your mum or dad clean your puppy's teeth, as they can be very sharp!

Puppies like to jump and catch balls. Throw a ball on the ground so it bounces high in the air and count how many bounces it makes before your puppy catches it. Use a ball that is not too big or too small for her. If she can't pick the ball up in her mouth, then it is too big. If she could swallow the ball then it is too small. Play this at your local park and you can bounce the ball really hard!

Anyone for rounders? Get a bat and ball and invite some friends around into your garden to play a game. Let your puppy be a fielder, which means he has to get the ball after you've hit it with the bat. If you can run around the course before your puppy brings the ball back, then you've scored, but if he catches the ball before it's hit the ground, you're out!

Play 'hunt the treat'! Try to get hold of some of your puppy's favourite treats without her knowing. Remember that she has good ears and can hear even the tiniest of rustling noises. Take two or three treats and hide them in a room where she can get to them easily. Call your puppy, let her sniff the smell of her treats on your hands, and then tell her to find them. See how long she takes.

When your puppy is old enough to go out for a walk, she will have to wear a collar and nametag. The collar will feel strange at first, so help her get used to it. Let her sniff it, then gently put it around her neck but don't do it up too tightly. If you can put two fingers between the collar and her neck, then it's just right. Keep checking her collar regularly as she grows up to make sure that it isn't getting too tight.

Do you go all goose-pimply when you are scared? Dogs do something similar when they are afraid. They raise their hackles, which means that all the fur on their backs stands up. If you are doing something that makes your puppy scared, then stop it immediately. Call him to you and give him a big hug or stroke to make him feel better.

As your puppy can't talk, it's important that you understand the noises she might make. When your puppy feels threatened for example, she might make a deep growling sound. If she's chewing a bone and thinks you might take it away from her, she might growl because she doesn't like that idea. It's her bone and not for anyone else. Don't go near your puppy if she's growling, but tell your mum or dad.

Your puppy's bark can mean lots of things, but if you listen carefully you can understand what he means. If he barks several times in his normal voice, he is trying to get your attention. Barking like this and sitting by the door usually means that he needs to go outside and have a wee. If he barks in a deeper voice, he's trying to tell you that he's seen somebody that he doesn't know and isn't sure if they are friendly or not.

Never try to train your puppy when you're in a bad mood. You're more likely to start shouting at her if she doesn't do what you want her to do. It's not your puppy's fault if you've had a bad day at school! Give her a hug instead and you'll soon start feeling better.

When your puppy is happy wearing a collar, you can get him used to wearing a lead. Take your puppy into the garden and put the lead on his collar, but don't hold on to it. Let it fall on the ground and allow your puppy to go around the garden pulling the lead behind him. Watch him carefully so that he doesn't tie himself up in knots!

There will be times when your puppy has to go to the vet's. Don't make him anxious by teasing him with the word 'vet's'. Instead, just go with your puppy so that you can keep him calm by stroking him and making a fuss of him. In the future, if your puppy has to go to the vet's after an accident, he won't be worried.

Look in a mirror and tell yourself off for doing something naughty. Now pull a happy face and say well done for being good. Can you see how your face changes? This is what your puppy sees when you tell her off or praise her. She doesn't understand the words you are saying but learns that a cross face means she's been bad and a happy face means she's been good. Show a happy face and she'll probably wag her tail.

Does your puppy have tickly feet? If you gently brush the fur between his pads with your finger, it feels the same as if you were having your feet tickled. Some dogs love this, but others hate it, so don't be surprised if your puppy stands up so you have to stop!

How good is your memory? Much better than your puppy's! If your puppy does something wrong, then say 'No' straight away. If she does something right, praise her immediately. This is how puppies learn. If you go shopping on a Saturday morning for three hours and come back to find your puppy's made a mess in the kitchen, you mustn't tell her off, because she won't know what she's done wrong. She'll have forgotten about the mess by now!

Puppies age quicker than humans.
How old is your puppy in dog years?
Every 'human year' is about the same
as seven 'dog years'. So when your
puppy is one year old, in dog years
he's really seven. It's a good way to
learn your seven times tables!

When you're on a long car journey, make sure that your puppy has plenty of room. Keep her calm and settled, and if she starts barking, make a fuss of her. If you could understand dog language, you'd probably find she's asking "Are we nearly there yet?"

Sandy beaches are great! When you're on holiday, always look for a sandy beach that dogs are allowed on. How good is your puppy at digging? See if you can get him to dig the moat for a huge sandcastle.

Does your puppy rip the newspaper to shreds as soon as the paperboy has delivered it, but before mum and dad have had a chance to read it? You'd better leave a note for Father Christmas telling him not to leave your presents on the floor under the Christmas tree. You don't want your puppy unwrapping them before you do!

Puppies love soft toys, so find one that your puppy can take to bed and cuddle. Check it closely to make sure that there's nothing sharp or loose on it that could harm him.

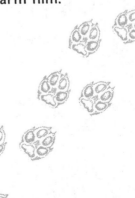

Your puppy is very clever, but there are some things that she will always need you to do. Check whether her drinking bowl needs more water adding to it, especially in the summer. If the bowl is too heavy for you to lift, leave it where it is. Instead, fill a beaker with cold water and pour that into the water bowl. Easy!

Teach your puppy some manners!
Train him to shake paws with people.
Say a command like "Paw", take one
of his front paws when he's sitting
up, and shake it as if you were
shaking hands. He'll soon start giving
you his paw when you ask for it.
Praise him when he does this.

Is your vet holding a puppy party?
Puppies mustn't go outside until
they've had all their injections, but at a
puppy party they can meet lots of
other people and puppies. It's a good
place for you and your puppy to make
new friends. Remember not to make
her jealous, though!

Your puppy might try to tell you
that he isn't feeling very well by
whining. This is a high-pitched noise
and sounds like he is crying. He
won't be wagging his tail, and if he
has ears that normally stand up,
they may be hanging down instead.
If you touch your puppy and he
suddenly yelps in a high-pitched
voice, then it probably hurts where
you touched him. A visit to the vet's
may be needed to make him better.

Your puppy has about 28 baby teeth.
These begin to fall out when she's
about 6 months old, when her 42
permanent teeth start growing. Your
puppy may become irritable because
her gums will be sore when her new
teeth start growing. Find her
something to chew - something hard
like a bone and something soft like a
soft toy are good. Then she can chew
on whichever feels more comfortable.

Have you been sitting in front of the television or playing computer games all day? Well, it's not good for you, and it isn't good for your puppy either. Go outside and play some games with him. Puppies need regular exercise. You'll both feel better for it, and be ready for your dinners!

How clean are your puppy's toys? The more she plays with them, the dirtier they get. Take a bowl of clean water outside and wash all the toys with a clean cloth. Give any soft toys to your mum or dad to clean in the washing machine. Make sure they're all dry before letting your puppy play with them again.

Bath time! When puppies get really dirty, the easiest place to clean them is in the bath. Let mum or dad do the washing, but ask if you can help. Put a rubber mat in the bottom of the bath to stop your puppy from sliding about, and don't use too much water. When you've finished, let the water out of the bath first. Then see who is wettest - you, your puppy or your mum or dad?

Dressing up can be fun! Put some tinsel around your puppy's collar at Christmas, or turn her into a superhero by draping a towel along her back. Hats and sunglasses don't always stay on though. If your puppy doesn't like it, don't force her to join in.

On wet days, dry your puppy's paws with his towel whenever he comes back indoors. If you don't, the mud on his paws may make him slip on the kitchen floor and hurt himself. Your mum might make you clean the kitchen floor afterwards if it's covered in dirty paw prints too!

Take care when you introduce your puppy to other pets you have at home. Always have mum or dad around in case your puppy gets too excited. A puppy can look big and frightening to a rabbit. Or perhaps your rabbit might scare your puppy! Don't let them out together in the garden until they've made friends with each other.

Your mum and dad will buy special puppy food because human food can be harmful to young puppies. So don't think that you can slip the vegetables you don't like under the table for your puppy to eat! When your puppy first comes to live with you he may have four meals every day. This is because he needs lots of nutrients and vitamins in order to grow properly. When he's one year old, your puppy will only need one meal a day.

Isn't snow great? It will seem strange to your puppy at first, so play with her in it so she learns that it's fun. Don't throw snowballs at her because they may hurt. Instead throw a snowball as you would any other ball and tell her to 'fetch' it. She may get confused when she can't find it in the snow! Build a snow puppy for your snowman, but don't play for too long. Snow can get trapped in your puppy's paws and make her feet very cold.

Fancy being a bit naughty? Pretend you and your puppy are in those television adverts for toilet rolls! Gently tie the end of the roll around your puppy's collar and see how far he can take the toilet paper around the house. Remember though that your mum and dad may not be amused if they go to the toilet and find an empty toilet roll...

There's a saying that goes
"A dog is for life, not just for Christmas",
which is very true. Make friends with your puppy and you've got a friend for life, not just until bedtime.